Winning Local

How to Build Your Brand and Dominate Your Target Market In 2024

Jeff Turnbow

This book contains the author's top tips for winning your local market and building your brand.

For a customized strategy based on your specific goals and market area, visit www.JeffTurnbow.com

Table of Contents

Preface

A current marketing revolution is happening for business and marketing in 2024. We are no longer just shifting but an evolution and revolution in marketing is happening right now. Today, it is more challenging than ever for businesses to establish a strategy and execute that strategy against the odds. That is where this book comes in.

"How to Win Local" is a guide for small to medium-sized businesses to compete in this new era. I will provide practical advice, easy-to-use steps, and proven strategies to help you establish your brand, plan your approach, choose your budget, focus on tactics, and build a strategic foundation for success. This book covers the most critical aspects of winning your target market.

THERE'S MARKETING,
THEN THERE'S *Winning!*

Acknowledgments

I'm so grateful to my kiddos - Altan, Toria, and Ava. My wonderful children have brought joy into my life that I had never imagined possible. They also teach me how to become more disciplined, determined, enthusiastic, and inspired. They are the biggest inspiration behind any of my success. My goal in life is to give them the best life possible and I am grateful that I get to achieve some of that by using my talents and passion for helping businesses.

All my family inspires me daily to be a better man, which impacts my work.

My amazing parents have passed on but their lessons about loyalty, work ethic, faith, and passion drive my business decisions daily.

My loving sisters and family who like every single post or project I touch inspire me to keep going and to never ever give up.

Mark and Carlene Hixson, Preston Rood, Dr. Carmella Knoernschild, Michael Knollmeyer, Joe Lacey, R.D. Walker, and all my longtime partners took a chance on allowing me to help steer their business and have continued for many years. I appreciate your continued trust more than you know. To my new partners, I thank you all for choosing me from the vast supply of options and beginning a journey of success together. I believe all my partnerships are very special connections from God. Loyalty and trust are withering values, but He continues to bless me with new partners who still believe in the value of partnerships, talent, experience, and loyalty.

Thank you to Aaron Polmeer, who put me on stages worldwide and shared my skills, talents, and strategies with your audiences.

To my Winning Local Crew who enables me to be the driver of our amazing company, thank you for each role you take in making this a winning company that helps create more winning companies.

To Zig Ziglar for just saying "You can have everything you want in life as long as you help enough other people get what they want". It is the golden rule of business.

Thank you to those investing your time to read this book. I truly hope it provides great value to your business.

Testimonials / Reviews

"Our revenues grew by over 100%!

We were throwing darts until Jeff got us on a strategy. Now, 8 years later, we are still partners with Jeff and Winning Local. Our revenues grew 100% within a short period. We especially enjoyed the more focused strategy and the website optimization and redesign have helped our site convert many more quality leads into sales."

**Mark Hixson, Owner
Southaven RV, and Marine**

"Jeff revolutionized our digital sales and marketing operations!"

**Tracey Rogers, VP
Raycom Media**

"I am beyond impressed with not only the quality of work but professionalism and the prompt service they deliver. Everything turned out perfectly and I will be using this company from here on out!!!"

Warren Martin
National Fitness Coach

"I am a small business owner. Winning Local built our store website and helped us get our new business open and ready to get customers. They helped with our logo, and menus, training our staff, and so much of getting us started. They are more than a marketing company - they are a business-building power team! I highly recommend this company!"

Crystal, Owner
Bobalicious Cafe

"Jeff Turnbow is one of the most qualified digital marketing professionals that I have worked with in my career. He is driven, successful, passionate about what he does, and is a leader in the industry. Jeff stays on the forefront of technology and stays ahead of the game with his clients. If you are looking to gain market share, Jeff is your guy!"

Heather Watson
Cox Media

"Professional, Knowledgeable, THE BEST & so much more! Had the pleasure of doing business with Winning Local for many years! Highly recommend them!"

Linsey Eakin
The Sparkled Leopard Boutique

"I have been doing business with Jeff for over 10 years now. He is very resolute and passionate about his job. His skill and expertise will take your business to a new level. I look forward to our journey through the next 10 years. I highly recommend Jeff Turnbow & Winning Local."

Joy Murphy, Owner
Dance with Joy Enterprises

"Jeff Turnbow has years of digital marketing experience. He has worked with businesses both large and small to increase their web traffic and digital visibility. Few other experts can match his results."

Courtney Lanning
Journalist, and Film Critic

"The sales training and strategy execution was exactly what we needed."

Jonathan Humphrey
United Welding Institute

"Our revenues grew 7X with Jeff and Winning Local. They are easy to communicate with and their marketing strategies are the best!

They are an amazingly talented team and if you want your business to grow, they are the Marketing company for you!!!"

Dr. Carmella Knoernschild, Orthodontist,
Owner, ClearlyDrK.com

Introduction:
David vs. Goliath - How Local Businesses Can Triumph

When I was growing up, one of the most profound stories that shaped my ideals about winning was the story of David and Goliath. This story has many powerful keys that we can begin and apply for underdogs that battle against competitors big and small.

David, a young shepherd, faced the giant Goliath, a fearsome warrior. Despite the odds stacked against him, David defeated Goliath with just a single stone and a sling. This story illustrates the potential for local businesses to succeed against larger competitors, even in a world where it seems they have many disadvantages.

Just like David, small business owners often rely on their ingenuity, faith, resourcefulness, and determination to succeed in the face of overwhelming competition. My father, a hardworking farmer, was no exception.

My father faced an uphill battle. I recall fond memories of watching him plow the fields and attending small farmer's associations. We often went for great food. He could not compete with the vast resources and economies of scale that the larger farmers had at their disposal. However, he did not let this deter him. Instead, he decided to focus on what he could control: his tools, equipment, work ethic, and passion for making a living for his family. His goals were different from other farmers and different from mine. I did not understand this at the time. I noticed he lacked the tools and resources to be more competitive during that time.

He did not have the larger tractor, providing the efficiency. He lacked the capital to invest. He lacked irrigation systems and often lived month to month on credit. However, he enjoyed his level of success, and it was sufficient to meet his goals.

He raised a family of five and we never felt that we lacked anything. When he passed, he left us a farm with no debt. That was success for him. I wanted him to have more, and he could have, but sometimes marketers miss the critical first step that is understanding their client's goal - how does the client define success?

He built strong relationships with customers and vendors, who appreciated the personal touch and superior products he offered. This dedication to quality, consistency, and customer service allowed him to not only survive but thrive in an increasingly competitive market. He didn't have a large number of customers, but he had excellent retention because he provided excellent quality and results.

He was a winner. He stopped farming on his own terms and therefore was a success. This was a real-life example for me. And even to this day, it serves as a testament to the power of setting proper goals, understanding your tools and resources, developing a strategy, and executing it properly.

If his goals were different, he could have leveraged his unique strengths and advantages, invested in tools and resources based on a proper plan and strategy, and become as successful as any other competitor. He had the passion, work ethic, and knowledge. With the right team and resources, I am confident he could have achieved any level of success he desired.

In the chapters that follow, we will explore various strategies, tools, and insights to help you reach the level of success that you desire.

We will delve into marketing tactics, customer relationship management, and other key factors that will enable you to effectively promote your products and services and meet your definition of success.

Turnbow Takeaways:

1. **Define Success. Set Goals. Plan. Gather your Resources:** Begin with the end in mind. Know what you want and chart your path. Some businesses want to simply maintain their market share while others want to dominate the market. Choose your team wisely and surround yourself with the best

resources possible. Create a strategy and execute the strategy.

2. **Focus on differentiation:** One of the key takeaways from this chapter is the importance of differentiation that sets your small business apart from competitors. Consider investing in the tools, equipment, or training necessary to provide a superior offering. By differentiating your business in this way, you can attract customers who are looking for something unique and are willing to pay a premium for it.

3. **Cultivate strong relationships with customers and vendors:** Building and maintaining strong relationships is crucial for small businesses looking to compete today, more than ever. Loyalty is a disappearing character. If you work with people, make wise choices, and be loyal to those who help you grow. Make

an effort to know your customers personally, understand their needs and deliver exceptional customer service.

By doing so, you will create a loyal customer base that will not only continue to patronize your business but purchase more often, and refer others to your business.

4. **Leverage your unique strengths:** As a business owner, identify the unique strengths that you and your business possess, which can give you a competitive edge over larger corporations. This may include your ability to make quick decisions, your local market knowledge, or your personalized approach to customer service.

Capitalize on these strengths and use them as part of your marketing strategy to highlight the benefits of choosing your business over a larger competitor. Often, a perceived weakness can be a strength. Smaller businesses can be more adaptive, agile, and attractive to customers who prefer their culture and environment.

What is your revenue goal for the next year?

What obstacles do you think hinder you from reaching your goal?

What would you do if you reach your goal?

What are your next steps to reach that goal?

Chapter 1:
Establishing Your Brand and Purpose

Why is it important for a local business to establish its brand and purpose?

In today's competitive market, it is more important than ever for local businesses to establish a strong brand identity and clearly defined purpose. A well-defined brand helps your business stand out from the competition and creates a lasting impression on your customers. Your purpose, on the other hand, is the foundation of your business, giving you direction and guiding your decision-making process. Together, a strong brand and purpose can help you attract and retain loyal customers, ultimately contributing to the growth and success of your business.

A great proverb tells us "Without vision, the people perish". Vision is the energy that creates purpose. Having a clear vision and identity allows your team to rally around more than a business. Employees need vision and purpose.

What is your vision for your company and what is your purpose in the marketplace?

In this chapter, we will share examples of how to move from vision and purpose towards creating a better selling proposition for your local business, ensuring that you communicate the problem you solve and how you solve it better than anyone else.

1. **Identify your target audience:** To create a compelling selling proposition, it is crucial to understand who your target customers are. This enables you to tailor your marketing efforts to the needs, preferences, and desires of those customers most likely to buy your product or service. By focusing your marketing efforts on a specific audience, you can optimize your marketing budget, increase customer satisfaction, and, grow your business. Here are a few steps to identify your target audience:

a. **Analyze your current customer base:** Start by examining your existing customers. Look for common characteristics and shared interests among them. Identifying patterns can help you understand the type of people who are most likely to be interested in your products or services.

If your business is new or doesn't have a large customer base yet, research your competitors and their customers to gain insights. If your business isn't new, you should still research your competition thoroughly. **What are their strengths, weaknesses, opportunities, and threats? What are yours?**

b. **Segment your audience:** Break down your potential customers into segments based on several factors, such as demographics (age, gender, income, education, etc.), geographic location, and psychographics (lifestyle, interests, values, etc.). This will help you create tailored marketing messages and campaigns for each segment, resulting in a more significant impact.

c. **Identify problems and needs:**
    Determine the specific problems or
    needs your product or service
    addresses. By understanding your
    customers' pain points, you can better
    position your business as the solution.

    For example, if you run a local bakery,
    your target audience might be people
    looking for fresh, high-quality baked
    goods made from locally sourced
    ingredients. Or you could serve those
    looking for gluten-free, low-carb, and
    healthier alternatives.

d. **Understand their purchasing behavior:**
    Study your target audience's buying
    habits, such as how they research and
    compare products, what factors
    influence their decision-making process,
    and where they prefer to shop.

    This can help you create marketing

strategies that cater to these preferences and habits, increasing the likelihood of conversion.

e. **Creating customer personas:** Develop detailed profiles or personas of your ideal customers, incorporating the insights gathered from the previous steps. These personas should represent the different segments within your target audience and include information about their demographics, psychographics, pain points, and purchasing behavior. Now you can better visualize your target audience and develop more targeted and effective marketing strategies.

According to Hubspot.com - Here is why you need to create a persona:

"A buyer persona extends beyond simply describing your audience; the powerful insights

generated by a buyer persona can be leveraged to make better business decisions.

Ultimately, a well-crafted buyer persona will help you understand your ideal customer and their goals, provide guidance on how to tailor your marketing strategy, guide product development, and help you prioritize your time.

When done well, buyer personas are incredibly valuable for marketing. They can help you find gaps in the content you create. You will also be able to use buyer personas to tailor your content so that it is relevant. Buyer personas can even help you figure out and spend."

We'll get more into using ads later, but for now, you should see that having a customer persona is incredibly important.

f. **The last step in identifying a target audience is to evaluate and refine:** Continually evaluate and adjust your target audience as you gain more insights from your marketing efforts and customer feedback. Be prepared to refine your target audience segments over time as your business evolves, and new trends emerge.

You will need to clearly articulate the problem you solve and the audience most impacted. **Clearly state the problem(s) your business solves and how it impacts your target audience:**

2. **Showcase your unique solution:** Explain how your products or services uniquely solve the problem you've identified. Highlight any innovative features, techniques, or methods that set you apart from your competitors and make your solution more effective or efficient.

3. **Share your story:** People love a delightful story, and your business's background can be an essential part of your selling proposition. Share how your business was founded, your motivations, and any challenges you've overcome to create an emotional connection with your customers.

   As I write this, I immediately think of a burger business. As you walk inside the business, there are black-and-white photos of the family. Customers can immediately sense the love and passion inside the business. There are photos of the father as a butcher boy at an early age. The story of quality ingredients and love of serving is immediately apparent.

4. **Offer social proof:** Build credibility by showcasing customer testimonials, reviews, or case studies that demonstrate the effectiveness of your

solution. This helps potential customers feel more confident in choosing your business over others. Today, business reviews influence purchase decisions more than ever. There are too many studies to support this. Studies are showing that when a business drops below a four-star, sales decrease by up to 20%.

By incorporating these elements into your selling proposition, you will effectively communicate the problem you solve, how you solve it, and why customers should choose your local business over the competition.

To conclude this chapter, here are your **Turnbow takeaways:**

1. A strong brand and purpose help local businesses stand out from the competition and attract loyal customers, making them vital for success.

2. Creating a compelling selling proposition involves understanding your target audience, articulating the problem you solve, displaying your unique solution, sharing your business's story, and offering social proof.

3. Use these techniques to craft a selling proposition that communicates the value of your business, setting you apart from competitors and resonating with your target audience.

What problem(s) do you solve?

How do you solve it better than your competition?

Say that in one sentence (without using the words: and, but, also)
Be as concise as possible.

Chapter 2:
Proper Planning- Know Your Capabilities and Capacity to Achieve Greatness

Why is it important for a local business to plan according to its resources?

Proper planning is the foundation of any successful business, and for local businesses, it's especially crucial to make plans according to their available resources. Many businesses start up or get caught up in the daily grind to the point of neglecting this vital step.

Efficient use of resources helps ensure that marketing efforts are targeted, cost-effective, and bring a high return on investment. It is important to analyze your capabilities and capacity.

In a marketing world with many platforms, tactics, strategies, and opportunities, local businesses must carefully understand what they can do <u>with greatness</u>. Are you a one-person team or do you have an entire marketing department? Or should you bring on a consultant/fractional CMO/Agency to extend your capabilities and capacity? This is so important.

With so much to do and keep up with, businesses must determine: What can I accomplish with my resources and do it GREAT? For example, I see many businesses trying to keep up with Google, Facebook, Instagram, Tik Tok, Pinterest, Websites, Blogs, and yet none of them are complete or have meaningful impact on growing or changing their business outcomes. With more limited capacity and capabilities, businesses must know how and concentrate their efforts towards the tactics they can do with profound impact. Do not get distracted by trying to do so much that nothing is done with greatness. This is often why businesses call me. They want help but they do not want a big company to handle their marketing - they're smart. They know that many large companies simply do not have the time and focus for their unique business needs. However, they still need to have more capabilities and capacity.

By carefully allocating resources such as time, money, and personnel, local businesses can stay competitive, even against larger corporations with more extensive resources. If you find yourself buying advertising on a whim or because you like the sales rep, you have fallen into this easy trap. If you lack the time to settle down, create a plan, and execute the plan, then it is time to bring on a trusted marketer. Marketing is vital and today it must be great.

Creating a winning marketing plan tailored to your business's resources involves research, goal setting, and strategic decision-making. Here is how to create an effective marketing plan for your local business:

1. **Conduct market research:** Start by researching your target audience, competitors, and industry trends. Understanding these factors will help you identify opportunities and challenges within your market and tailor your marketing efforts accordingly. Remember, this changes, so it must be optimized often.

2. **Set clear goals and objectives:** Establish specific, measurable, achievable, relevant, and time-bound **(SMART)** goals for your marketing efforts. These goals

might include increasing brand awareness, driving sales, or attracting new customers. Clearly defined goals will help you focus your resources on initiatives that directly contribute to your desired outcomes.

3. **Develop a marketing budget:** Based on your available resources, create a realistic marketing budget that will help you achieve your goals. Allocate funds to different marketing channels, keeping in mind the cost-effectiveness and potential impact of each channel. Be wise about marketing budget. This is the fuel to the engine of your business.

   A quick Google search will tell you to invest 2-10% of your gross sales on marketing. Most suggest 10%. I know that doesn't help much. However, it is a scale, and it is very much relative to many variables: **What are your goals?**

Are you new or dominant in your market? Are you losing to a competitor? What is your expected ROI? What are your resources? These answers can move the scale to one end or the other.

4. **Which marketing tactics:** Based on your research and budget, select the marketing tactics that will best help you reach your target audience and achieve your goals. These may include social media marketing, paid search, email marketing, content marketing, or even local events and sponsorships. If your budget is small, this list will be small – because if you choose a tactic, then it should be executed with greatness and impact.

5. **Create a marketing calendar:** Develop a timeline for implementing your marketing initiatives, including specific

deadlines and milestones. A marketing calendar will help you stay organized, allocate resources effectively, and ensure your marketing efforts are consistent and well-coordinated. It can change, but at least have a plan.

6. **Monitor, measure, and adjust:** Track the performance of your marketing efforts, using key performance indicators (KPIs) relevant to your goals. **Are you measuring clicks, calls, purchases, reviews, opportunities, etc.?** Regularly review your marketing plan to identify areas of success and areas that may require adjustments. Be prepared to adapt your marketing strategies based on your findings and changes in your business environment.

With these steps, you can develop a marketing plan that caters to your unique resources. By doing so, you can ensure that your marketing endeavors are effective, focused, and prosperous.

"Concentration is the key to all economic success." - Peter Drucker

This philosophy emphasizes the importance of focusing on a few key areas rather than spreading resources too thin across many initiatives. In the context of marketing, this means that businesses should concentrate their efforts on a select few marketing tactics, rather than attempting to cover too many which often dilutes the impact of the marketing.

Focusing on a limited number of marketing tactics allows businesses to more impactful with the tactics that are most effective for their specific target audience and goals. This focused approach has several advantages over spreading the budget thinly across too many tactics:

1. **Concentration:** By concentrating on a few marketing strategies, businesses can develop a deeper understanding of each tactic's nuances and best practices. This expertise enables them to implement more effective campaigns, leading to better results.

2. **More efficient resource allocation:** Focused marketing allows businesses to allocate their resources more efficiently. Rather than spreading their budget across multiple tactics, they can invest more heavily into the ones that have the highest potential return on investment (ROI). This helps maximize the effectiveness of their marketing efforts while minimizing waste.

3. **Clearer messaging:** When businesses focus on a select few marketing tactics, they can more easily develop a consistent and coherent message that

resonates with their target audience. In contrast, dabbling in too many tactics can lead to fragmented messaging, wasting time, and diluting the brand's overall impact.

4. **Easier measurement and optimization:** By concentrating on a few marketing strategies, businesses can more easily measure the performance of each tactic and make data-driven decisions to optimize their campaigns. This can be challenging when resources are spread thin across multiple tactics, making it difficult to accurately assess the effectiveness of each one.

5. **Stronger competitive advantage:** Focused marketing efforts can help businesses build a competitive advantage in their chosen tactics. By honing their skills in specific areas, they can outperform competitors who are

spreading their efforts too thin. This strategy will lead to more visibility, more results, increased market share, and brand recognition. This is the principle of concentration I have applied to business marketing for over twenty years for over 200 types of businesses and it works!

To conclude, here are the 3 key **Turnbow Takeaways:**

1. Proper planning is essential for local businesses to make the most of their resources, ensuring efficient and effective marketing efforts that can compete against larger corporations.

2. Creating a marketing plan involves conducting market research, setting SMART goals, developing a budget, choosing marketing channels and tactics, creating a marketing calendar, and monitoring performance.

3. Following these steps will help you develop a marketing plan tailored to your available resources, setting your business up for greater efficiencies and more effective impact.

S PECIFIC

M EASURABLE

A CHIEVABLE

R ELEVANT

T IME-BOUND

Chapter 3:
Build Your Best Foundation

So many businesses run too fast failing to build a solid foundation. Many new businesses do not spend proper time on their signage, website, Google local listings, and social media presence before launching. Building a solid foundation for your local business is crucial to ensuring long-term success. I often meet with businesses often who are moving along while the foundation is not properly secured.

Before investing heavily into advertising, it is important to have the foundational elements in place, such as attractive signage, a well-designed website (to convert traffic into leads/sales), SEO, a complete and accurate Google listing, and a great social media presence.

Establishing these elements will not only help create a positive first impression for potential customers but also enhance the effectiveness of your advertising efforts, ensuring that you get the most out of your marketing budget.

Focusing on your business's foundation before launching an extensive advertising campaign allows you to:

1. **Create a consistent brand:** By developing your unique selling proposition, signage, website, Google listing, and social media presence before advertising, you can ensure that your

brand image is consistent across all channels. This consistency is crucial for building brand recognition and trust among your target audience.
Remember, there is nothing like great advertising to kill a brand. This means that if you launch a big campaign only to push visitors to a poor presence, it could create more harm than good. Make certain you have the proper foundation before opening the floodgates.

2. **Optimize the customer experience:** A well-designed website and accurate Google listing provide potential customers with the information they need to make informed decisions about your products or services. Similarly, an active social media presence enables you to engage with customers, answer their questions, and showcase the personality of your business.

By focusing on these elements before launching an advertising campaign, you can optimize the customer experience and increase the likelihood of converting potential customers into loyal patrons. Prospects will research you. Do not let them find a blank Google listing, no reviews, or social media pages with old content. Don't drive them to a location or web presence where the experience does not depict your desired experience. Don't drive them to a site where it is not prepared to convert.

3. **Maximize the impact of your advertising efforts:** With a solid foundation in place, your advertising campaigns will be more effective. When potential customers see your ads and decide to visit your website, Google listing, or social media profiles, they will encounter a well-designed, informative, and engaging experience, which helps

drive conversions and build customer loyalty.

Start with creating a visually appealing and informative website. This website should be easy to navigate, mobile-friendly, and optimized for search engines (BASIC SEO). Most importantly, the site should be designed by someone who understands conversion optimization – meaning the site is prepared and assessed to convert visitors into customers.

Alongside the website, ensure that your Google local listing is accurate and up-to-date, including contact information, hours of operation, details, and high-quality images. Next, create branded social media profiles on platforms relevant to your target audience and begin sharing engaging content that showcases your products, services, and company culture.

By focusing on these foundational elements before launching a large-scale advertising campaign, you can ensure that your business is well-positioned to capitalize on the increased visibility and traffic generated by your marketing efforts.

What is Sun Tzu's "The Art of War"?

Sun Tzu's "The Art of War" is an ancient Chinese military strategy that has been widely studied and applied in various fields, including business marketing. The timeless principles it contains can offer valuable insights into strategic thinking and competition in the business world. Here are Sun Tzu's five famous quotes about war and strategy, along with explanations of how they apply to compete as a business:

1. *"The supreme art of war is to subdue the enemy without fighting."*

In business, this quote suggests that the most effective strategy is to achieve success without engaging in direct competition. By finding unique ways to differentiate your products or services, you can create a competitive advantage without needing to engage in price wars or other direct aggressive competition. This could include focusing on niche markets, offering exceptional customer service, or innovating in ways that make your offerings stand out from the competition.

2. *"All warfare is based on deception."*

In the context of business, this quote emphasizes the importance of staying ahead of competitors by keeping your strategies and intentions hidden. This can involve protecting your trade secrets, being discreet about upcoming product launches, or using misdirection to keep competitors guessing about your next moves. By maintaining an element of surprise, you can catch your competitors off guard and gain a competitive advantage.

3. *"If you know the enemy and know yourself, you need not fear the result of a hundred battles."*

This quote highlights the importance of understanding both your own business and that of your competitors. By conducting thorough market research and competitor analysis, you can identify the strengths and weaknesses of both your own company and your rivals. This knowledge will enable you to develop strategies that capitalize on your strengths, exploit your competitors' weaknesses, and achieve success in the market.

4. *"Opportunities multiply as they are seized."*

In business, this quote suggests that taking advantage of opportunities can lead to further opportunities down the line. By being initiative-taking and seizing market opportunities as they arise, your business can gain momentum, attract new customers, and create a positive feedback loop that drives further growth. This could involve launching new products, expanding into new markets, or forming strategic partnerships to strengthen your position in the industry. Smaller businesses can often move quicker and therefore seize opportunities much faster than larger competitors.

5. *"Amid the chaos, there is also opportunity."*

This quote reminds us that challenging situations can also present opportunities for businesses that are prepared to adapt and innovate. Economic downturns, industry disruptions, and other chaotic events can create openings for businesses that are flexible, agile, and able to pivot in response to changing circumstances. By staying alert to new opportunities and being willing to change course when needed, businesses can thrive even in the face of adversity.

In summary, Sun Tzu's famous quotes about war and strategy can be applied to the world of business to help guide strategic thinking and competition. By embracing these principles, businesses can develop effective strategies that enable them to differentiate themselves from competitors, seize opportunities, and adapt to the ever-changing business landscape.

To conclude this chapter, here are 3 key Turnbow Takeaways:

1. Building a solid foundation for your local business, including your unique selling proposition (what you do better), signage, website, Google listing, and

social media, is crucial for maximizing the impact of your advertising efforts and ensuring long-term success.

2. Focusing on fine-tuning foundational elements before launching an advertising campaign helps create a consistent brand image, optimize the customer experience, and drive conversions.

Chapter 4:
Utilizing Free Tools

As local businesses face fierce competition and tight budgets, finding cost-effective marketing

strategies is crucial for success. Guerrilla-style marketing tactics, which are creative, unconventional, and often low-cost, gained popularity in 2021 as businesses sought to maximize their marketing impact.

Here are my current top ten guerrilla marketing tactics:

1. **Social media contests:** Hosting contests on platforms like Facebook, Instagram, and Twitter can boost engagement, increase brand awareness, and grow your online following. Offer valuable prizes that are relevant to your business and encourage participants to share your content with their networks.

2. **Collaborations and partnerships:** Partner with complementary local businesses to cross-promote each other's products or services. This can be a win-win situation, as both businesses

benefit from increased exposure and potential new customers.

3. **Local event sponsorships:** Sponsoring local events, such as charity fundraisers, community gatherings, or sports teams/competitions, can raise your brand's local profile while showing your commitment to the community.

4. **Public art and installations:** Creating eye-catching public art or installations can help your business stand out and generate buzz. This could include murals, sculptures, or displays and designs that showcase your brand's creativity and personality.

5. **Influencer marketing:** Collaborate with local influencers who have a good online following. In exchange for free products or services, influencers will often share their experience with your brand,

reaching a wider audience and potentially driving new customers to your business. Remember, in a local market, you do not need celebrities. Everyone is a potential influencer.

6. **Pop-up shops and live events:** Organize temporary pop-up shops or events to create a sense of urgency and excitement around your products or services. This can help attract new customers, generate buzz, and provide a unique experience that sets your business apart.

7. **QR Codes:** QR Codes went away and came back strong during covid. Most people are now familiar with them, and you can use them alongside a question, contest, or problem to drive people to the solution or site to convert them into a lead or sale.

8. **Promotional items:** Design eye-catching stickers or gifts featuring your brand logo or a catchy phrase and distribute them with a strategy. For example, design contests with promotional items you know that your audience will use often. This can help increase brand recognition and serve as a conversation starter.

9. **Local search engine optimization (SEO):** Optimize your website and Google My Business listing to improve your visibility in local search results. This can help attract more local customers who are searching for products or services like yours. Submit your site to search engines. Look for or ask a marketer for tips on optimizing your site and Google listing to move it higher on page one.

10. **Content marketing:** Create valuable, informative, and engaging content that

appeals to your target audience. Share this content on your website, blog, and social media channels to establish your brand as an authority in your industry, drive website traffic, and generate leads.

By incorporating these guerrilla-style marketing tactics into your marketing plan, you can effectively promote your local business without a large financial investment. Remember to be creative, think outside the box, and utilize free or low-cost tools to make the most of your marketing efforts.

How to Set up a Google My Business Profile?

Setting up a Google My Business (GMB) profile is essential for local businesses, as it helps improve your online presence, increase your visibility in local search results, and provide potential customers with valuable information about your business. Here's a step-by-step guide on how to set up your Google Local Business profile:

1. **Create a Google account:** If you don't already have a Google account, you'll need to create one at https://accounts.google.com/signup. If you have an existing Google account, sign in and proceed to the next step.

2. **Go to Google My Business:** Visit https://www.google.com/business/ and click on the "Sign in" button in the top right corner. Sign in with your Google account.

3. **Start the setup process:** Once you are signed in, click on the "Manage now" button to begin setting up your GMB profile.

4. **Enter your business name:** Type in the name of your business and click "Next." If your business already has a GMB profile, you will be prompted to claim it. If not, you will proceed to create a new listing.

5. **Choose your business category:** Select the category that best describes your business. This is important, as it helps Google determine which search queries your business should appear for. Make sure to choose the most accurate and specific category for your business.

6. **Add your business location:** Enter your business address and click "Next." If your business does not have a physical location (e.g., you are a service-based business serving customers at their locations), you can select "I deliver goods and services to my customers" and define your service area.

7. **Set your service area (if applicable):** If you selected "I deliver goods and services to my customers" in the previous step, you will be prompted to define your service area by adding regions, cities, or postal codes. This helps Google show your business to customers in those areas.

8. **Provide contact information:** Add your business phone number and website URL. If you do not have a website, you can select "I don't need a website" or choose to create a free website with Google My Business.

9. **Verify your listing:** To confirm that you are authorized to manage the business listing, Google will require you to verify your listing. You can choose from several verification options, including postcard, phone, email, or instant verification (if eligible). Follow the instructions for your

chosen method to complete the verification process.

10. **Complete your profile:** After verification, you can add more details to your GMB profile, such as business hours, photos, a business description, and more. The more information you provide, the more helpful your listing will be to potential customers.

By setting up your Google Local Business profile correctly, you will make it easier for potential customers to find your business, learn about your products or services, and get in touch with you. Be sure to keep your GMB listing up to date with accurate information and engage with customers by responding to reviews and posting updates regularly.

Many businesses have a Facebook page but still have not used Instagram. I encourage this especially since they are owned by the same company, and you can post or advertise to both at the same time within their platform. Setting up an Instagram account for your business will help you connect with your target audience, display your products or services, and build your brand. This can be operated like a 2-for-1 opportunity.

Here is a step-by-step guide on how to set up an Instagram account properly:

1. **Download the Instagram app:** Download the Instagram app from the App Store (iOS) or Google Play Store (Android) and install it on your smartphone or tablet.

2. **Sign up for an account:** Open the Instagram app and tap "Sign Up" or "Create New Account." You can either sign up with your email address, phone number or log in with an existing Facebook account. If you choose to sign

up with an email address or phone number, you will need to verify your account through a confirmation code sent to your email or phone.

3. **Create a username and password:** Choose a username that reflects your business name or brand and is easy to remember. Create a strong, secure password to protect your account.

4. **Switch to a business account:** Once you have signed up for an account, it's important to switch to a business account, as it offers additional features such as analytics, contact options, and the ability to run ads. To switch to a business account, follow these steps:

   a. Tap the profile icon in the bottom right corner of the app.

b. Tap the three horizontal lines (the menu icon) in the top right corner.

c. Select "Settings" from the menu.

d. Tap "Account."

e. Scroll down and select "Switch to Professional Account."

f. Choose "Business" and follow the prompts to complete the setup process.

5. Complete your profile: Add a profile picture that represents your business, such as your logo or an image of your storefront. Write a clear and concise bio that describes your business and highlights your unique selling points. You can also include relevant hashtags or emojis, as well as a link to your website or a specific landing page.

6. Connect other social media accounts: If you have other social media accounts for your business, such as Facebook, Twitter, or LinkedIn, you can connect them to your Instagram account. This will allow you to share your Instagram content across multiple platforms. To connect other accounts, go to "Settings," then "Account," and finally "Sharing to Other Apps."

7. Develop a content strategy: Plan the type of content you want to share on your Instagram account, such as product photos, behind-the-scenes glimpses, customer testimonials, or promotional offers. Determine a consistent posting schedule and create a content calendar to stay organized.

8. Use hashtags and geotags: Incorporate relevant hashtags and geotags in your posts to increase your visibility and reach potential customers. Research popular and trending hashtags in your industry or niche and use a mix of broad and specific hashtags. You can get this in the Meta Business Suite where Facebook and Instagram are combined.

9. Engage with your audience: Respond to comments, messages, and mentions to build a relationship with your followers. Engage with other accounts in your industry or niche by liking, commenting, and sharing their content. Sharing other people's content will usually encourage people to share your content. Also, within a smaller community, you show that you love and care about your community.

10. Analyze and optimize: Regularly review your Facebook and Instagram analytics, which is available on business accounts, to track your account's performance, identify trends, and make data-driven decisions to optimize your content strategy.

This can appear easy, and it is if you are a small business in a very small market. However, this is also a very powerful tactic that a professional marketer can use to create tremendous success for your business. You may find yourself spending too much time here or not getting desired results. That is the time to ask a pro.

Best Practices for Optimized Website Homepage Results

Optimizing your website's homepage for conversions, such as phone calls or purchases, and search engine optimization (SEO) is crucial to attracting potential customers and encouraging them to take action.

Here are the best practices for optimizing your homepage:

1. **Clear and concise headline:** Your homepage should have a clear and compelling headline that communicates

your value proposition and captures the visitor's attention immediately. Make sure it highlights the primary purpose of your product or service and how you address your target audience's needs or pain points - **uniquely.**

2. **Easy-to-find contact information:** Display your phone number prominently on your homepage, preferably in the header or top navigation, so that visitors can easily find it and make a call. You can also add a click-to-call feature, allowing mobile users to call your business directly from your website. No, customers do not want to search at all for contact information.

3. **Strong call-to-action (CTA):** Include a strong and clear CTA that encourages visitors to take the desired action, such as making a purchase or signing up for a newsletter, contest, discount club, etc.

Make sure the CTA button is visually distinct, uses actionable language, and is placed in a prominent location on your homepage.

4. **Mobile responsiveness:** Ensure your website is mobile-friendly, as more users access websites on mobile devices than desktop computers. A responsive design ensures that your website looks and functions well on different devices and screen sizes, providing a positive user experience and improving your search engine rankings.

5. **Page speed:** Optimize your website's loading speed, as slow-loading pages can frustrate visitors and negatively impact your search engine rankings. Compress images, minify CSS and JavaScript files, and leverage browser caching to improve page speed.

6. **User-friendly navigation:** Organize your website's navigation intuitively, making it easy for visitors to find important information and explore your site. Use descriptive navigation labels and include a search bar to help users quickly find what they're looking for.

7. **Quality content:** Provide valuable, informative, and engaging content on your homepage that addresses your target audience's needs, interests, or pain points. Use clear and concise language, and break up large blocks of text with headings, bullet points, or visuals to make it easily digestible.

8. **On-page SEO:** Implement on-page SEO best practices, such as using relevant keywords in your title tag, meta description, header tags, and content. However, avoid keyword stuffing and focus on creating high-quality, natural-

sounding content that provides value to your users. Think: How will the visitor perceive this information, and will it make them want to take action?

9. **Visual elements:** Use high-quality images and visuals to support your content and create a visually appealing homepage. Ensure that your images are optimized for web use to avoid slowing down your page speed.

10. **Social proof:** Display testimonials, reviews, or case studies on your homepage to showcase the positive experiences of your customers and build trust with potential clients. You can also highlight any industry awards, certifications, or media mentions to further establish your credibility.

By following these best practices, you can optimize your website's homepage for both conversions and SEO, making it more likely that visitors will take the desired action and improve your visibility in search engine results.

Remember to regularly analyze your website's performance, track user behavior, and make data-driven adjustments to continually improve your homepage optimization.

Just as a brick and mortar requires constant maintenance, updates, and improvements, so does your web presence. In fact, it is more important if I had to choose.

Turnbow Takeaways:

1. Guerrilla marketing tactics can help local businesses maximize their marketing impact on a tight budget, using creative

and unconventional strategies to capture attention and generate buzz.

2. Home page optimization is critical to turning visitors into customers.

3. Mobile first. Optimize your site for mobile as this will be the most popular device for your visitors.

4. Optimize your site for basic SEO. If you build it yourself, you can accomplish these goals. If you hire a website designer, they should also be experienced in SEO. ALL OUR SITES COME WITH SEO AND GOOGLE LOCAL OPTIMIZATION AT www.WinningLocal.com

5. Always analyze and optimize. You can always improve a website. Study user behavior on your site to learn what they want and give it to them. Also, show the

customer where you want them to go within seconds of their arrival. Give them options to select to communicate with you and place them in multiple locations. Give a clear call to action such as "Sign Up for Deals", "Get Inventory Updates", "Get Your Free Trial", "Speak to a Specialist Now", "Get Your Free Report", etc.

Chapter 5:
The Art and Science of Advertising

In today's highly competitive market, advertising plays a pivotal role in the success of any business. It is both an art and a science, requiring a perfect blend of creativity, intuition, experience, psychology, and data-driven decision-making.

This chapter will delve into the essential aspects of advertising and help you understand the art and science behind it.

Just as an exceptional artist understands the proper paints, brushes, and techniques, so does the great marketer. Also, understanding the science and data, helps the creativity achieve the best and continuous results.

1. **The Art of Advertising:** At its core, advertising is about telling a compelling story that resonates with your target audience and creates an action. It demands a deep understanding of human emotions, desires, and needs to craft messages that captivate and persuade. The art of advertising involves the following:

   a. Creativity: Successful advertising campaigns are innovative, unique, and memorable. They capture the audience's attention, evoke emotions, and create an impression.

   b. Visual Appeal: Visually striking advertisements are more likely to grab attention and make a lasting impact. Combining powerful visuals with compelling copywriting helps create ads that resonate with the audience. Perform A/B testing on copywriting. For example, run a test ad on social media that has a direct approach while also running an ad with a more creative copy. Use the one that gets the best response then test it against another creative copy -and so on and so on. This helps you refine your ads to what works for your audience vs. what you think will work.

c. Emotional Connection: Emotional advertising is powerful. By evoking feelings of joy, fear, trust, or nostalgia, ads can create a deep connection with consumers and inspire action.

2. **The Science of Advertising:** Advertising is also a data-driven discipline that relies on research, analytics, and insights to inform decision-making and optimize campaigns. The science of advertising involves the following:

a. Market Research: Understanding your target audience, their preferences, and behaviors is crucial for creating effective advertisements. Conduct market research to gather insights that inform your advertising strategy.

b. Media Planning: Select the right media channels/tactics for your ads, based on your target audience, budget, and campaign objectives. Consider factors such as reach, frequency, and cost-effectiveness when making media buying decisions. Frequency can often be more important than reach. Remember that we are seeing thousands of ads every day. Your ad will usually need to be viewed 6-9 times before the viewer acts.

c. Measurement and Optimization: Analyze the performance of your advertising campaigns to identify areas for improvement. Track key metrics, such as impressions, clicks, conversions, and return on investment (ROI), and make data-driven adjustments to optimize your campaigns.

3. **Balancing Art and Science:** The most successful advertising campaigns strike a balance between art and science. They combine powerful stories, copy, and emotional appeal with data-driven insights and strategic decision-making. To achieve this balance:

   a. Collaborate: Encourage collaboration between creative and data-driven teams, fostering an environment where ideas and insights are shared freely.

   b. Test and Learn: Continuously experiment with different creative approaches, media channels, and targeting options.

Learn from the results and iterate on your campaigns to achieve the best possible outcomes.

c. Stay Informed: Keep up with industry trends, emerging technologies, and consumer preferences. Adapt your advertising strategies to stay relevant and effective in a constantly changing landscape.

Free Publicity

1. **Leverage Local Media:** Reach out to local newspapers, radio stations, and television channels, as they are often interested in covering stories about local businesses and community events. Pitch a newsworthy story about your business, such as a product launch, charity event, or an interesting backstory. Building relationships with

local journalists and editors can increase your chances of getting free coverage.

2. **Collaborate with Influencers and Bloggers:** Partner with influencers or bloggers within your industry who have a strong following and are relevant to your target audience. Offer them free samples of your product, exclusive access to your services, or valuable content that their audience will find useful.

   In return, they may promote your business through their social media channels, blog posts, or other content, giving you free exposure to a wider audience.

3. **Engage with Your Community:** Participate in local events, sponsor community initiatives, or host workshops and seminars related to your

industry. Engaging with your community not only helps build your reputation but also increases the chances of being covered by local media or gaining word-of-mouth publicity.

Actively contribute to online community forums and social media groups by providing valuable insights, answering questions, or sharing relevant content.

4. **Utilize Social Media:** Social media platforms like Facebook, Instagram, Twitter, and LinkedIn can be powerful tools for gaining free publicity. Create and share engaging, informative, and share-worthy content that highlights your expertise, highlights your products, or services, and resonates with your target audience.

Use hashtags and participate in industry-related conversations to increase your visibility. Encourage satisfied customers to leave reviews and testimonials on social media, as positive feedback can help attract new customers and boost your credibility.

Publish Press Releases: Write and distribute press releases to announce newsworthy events or milestones related to your business.

Press releases can catch the attention of journalists and editors, leading to media coverage and increased publicity.

Distribute your press releases through free or low-cost press release distribution services or send them directly to journalists and editors who cover your industry.

Make sure your press release is well-written, concise, and focuses on the most newsworthy aspects of your announcement.

By implementing these five straightforward ways to get free publicity, you can raise awareness about your business, reach a wider audience, and build a positive reputation, all without spending a fortune on advertising.

Turnbow Takeaways:

- Advertising is both an art and a science, requiring a balance between creativity, emotional appeal, and data-driven insights.

- Successful advertising campaigns are built on thorough market research, strategic media planning, and continuous measurement and optimization.

- Encourage collaboration between creative and analytical teams, embrace experimentation, and stay informed about industry trends to create impactful advertising campaigns that resonate with your target audience and drive results.

GEOGRAPHIC

region, city, country, culture,
weather, economy

PSYCHOGRAPHICS

lifestyle, personailty traits
hobbies, values

DEMOGRAPHIC

age, gender, occupations,
status, income, education

BEHAVIOUR

date, time, number of
purchases, occasions, habits

Chapter 6:
Getting to Know Your Buyers

Once upon a time, in a small town, there lived a passionate baker named Tom. He had a dream to open his bakery and share his love for baking with the community. Tom invested his savings, worked tirelessly to perfect his recipes, and finally opened "Tom's Tasty Treats."

In the beginning, Tom believed that everyone in town would be interested in his delicious baked goods. He spent a significant portion of his budget on advertising, trying to reach as many people as possible. He placed ads in local newspapers, put up billboards, and ran promotions on social media.

Despite his efforts, the bakery struggled to attract a steady stream of customers. Tom was disheartened by the lack of response and knew he needed to change his approach. He decided to consult a marketing expert named Sarah, who recommended that he define his target customer instead of marketing to everyone.

Tom and Sarah began by conducting market research and analyzing the bakery's existing customer base. They discovered that Tom's most loyal customers were young families who appreciated quality, homemade baked goods for special occasions and weekend treats. This demographic valued the bakery's use of natural, locally sourced ingredients and its commitment to traditional baking methods.

With this newfound understanding of his target audience, Tom revamped his marketing strategy. He focused on creating content that would resonate with young families, highlighting the bakery's wholesome, artisanal values. Tom highlighted his unique selling points: personalized service, high-quality ingredients, and the delightful experience of enjoying freshly baked goods with loved ones.

Tom also optimized his advertising efforts by targeting where his ideal customers were most likely to be found and with frequency. He began sponsoring local family events, offering baking workshops for parents and children, and collaborating with mommy bloggers and influencers in the parenting niche.

As Tom's marketing efforts became more targeted and focused, his bakery gained traction. Word-of-mouth spread among the young families in the community, and soon, "Tom's Tasty Treats" became the go-to place for birthday cakes, holiday treats, and weekend indulgences.

Tom's success grew exponentially as he continued to cater to the needs and desires of his target audience. He expanded his bakery to include a cozy seating area where families could enjoy their treats and spend quality time together. Tom even introduced a line of allergy-friendly and gluten-free options to accommodate the diverse needs of his customers.

By defining his target customer and adjusting his marketing strategy accordingly, Tom was able to turn "Tom's Tasty Treats" into a thriving, beloved bakery in the community. His story serves as a powerful reminder of the importance of understanding your audience and focusing your marketing efforts on those who will genuinely appreciate and value what your business has to offer – constantly optimizing your entire business.

Understanding your buyers is an essential aspect of a successful marketing strategy. By getting to know your target audience, you can create personalized, targeted campaigns that resonate with them and yield better results. In this chapter, we will explore the importance of personas, psychographics, and demographics in getting to know your buyers.

1. **Buyer Personas:** A buyer persona is a semi-fictional representation of your ideal customer, based on market research and existing customer data. It includes details about their demographics, psychographics, goals, challenges, and purchasing behavior. Creating buyer personas helps you:

   a. Tailor your messaging: By understanding your ideal customer's pain points and desires, you can create marketing messages that address their needs and highlight the benefits of your products or services.

b. Develop targeted campaigns:
Knowing your target audience enables
you to create marketing campaigns that
resonate with them and are more likely
to convert.

c. Improve product or service offerings:
Understanding your customer's needs,
preferences, and expectations can help
you refine and improve your products or
services.

2. **Psychographics:** Psychographics refers
to the qualitative aspects of your target
audience, such as their values, interests,
attitudes, and lifestyle. Gaining insights
into these aspects can help you:

   a. Create emotional connections: By
   understanding your audience's values
   and interests, you can create marketing
   messages that appeal to their emotions
   and create deeper connections.

b. Segment your audience:
Psychographics can be used to segment your audience into smaller groups with similar interests, allowing for more targeted and personalized marketing campaigns.

c. Identify opportunities: Understanding the attitudes and motivations of your target audience can help you identify opportunities for new products, services, or marketing tactics.

3. **Demographics:** Demographics refer to the quantitative aspects of your target audience, such as their age, gender, income, education, and location. Demographic data is useful for the following:

a. Defining your target market:
Demographics help you identify the specific group of people who are most

likely to be interested in your products or services.

b. Creating targeted campaigns: Demographic data can be used to tailor your marketing campaigns to the preferences and needs of different audience segments.

c. Allocating resources: Understanding the demographics of your target audience can help you allocate your marketing resources more effectively, by focusing on the channels and tactics that are most likely to reach them.

Turnbow Takeaways:

- Buyer personas, psychographics, and demographics are essential tools to know your buyers, enabling you to create targeted and personalized marketing campaigns.

- Use buyer personas to understand your ideal customers' needs, preferences, and pain points, and tailor your messaging accordingly.

- Consider both psychographic and demographic factors when segmenting your audience, to ensure your marketing campaigns are relevant and resonate with your target customers.

Chapter 7:
Understanding ROI

As a local business, understanding ROI (return on investment) is critical to achieving success. ROI is the ratio of the profit of an investment to the cost of the investment.

For a local business, ROI can be applied to marketing and advertising efforts, and it helps business owners understand which marketing strategies are delivering the most value for their money.

Marketing and Advertising Data

To understand ROI, a local business needs to track and analyze key performance indicators (KPIs) for its marketing and advertising campaigns. KPIs are metrics that provide insight into the effectiveness of marketing efforts. Some of the most important KPIs include cost per click (CPC), cost per lead (CPL), and cost per sale (CPS).

CPC is the amount of money a business pays for each click on its ad. CPL is the cost of generating a lead, while CPS is the cost of generating a sale.

By tracking these metrics, a local business can understand how much they are spending on each marketing or advertising effort and how much revenue they are generating from each campaign.

Return on Advertising Investment

Return on advertising investment (ROAI) is another important metric for local businesses. It is the ratio of the revenue generated by an advertising campaign to the cost of that campaign.

To calculate ROAI, a business needs to know the revenue generated from the campaign and the total cost of the campaign, including ad spend, creative costs, and any other related expenses.

By understanding ROAI, a local business can determine which advertising campaigns are generating the most revenue and adjust their marketing strategy accordingly. This data allows businesses to focus their efforts on the most profitable campaigns and allocate their resources more effectively.

Turnbow Takeaways:

1. Understanding ROI helps local businesses determine the effectiveness of their marketing and advertising campaigns.

2. Tracking KPIs like CPC, CPL, and CPS allows businesses to analyze the cost-effectiveness of their marketing efforts.

3. By calculating ROAI, a local business can determine which advertising campaigns are generating the most revenue and adjust their marketing strategy accordingly.

Chapter 8:
Wow Customer Service

In today's business world, local businesses are often faced with competition from larger companies with significant resources and brand recognition. One of the keyways that local businesses can differentiate themselves from these larger competitors is by providing excellent customer service.

Brand loyalty is fading as increased options flood the consumer. This makes constant and consistent Wow service more important than ever before. You can no longer rely on simply good customer service. Bad customer service will quickly damage your sales and ultimately your entire brand. Customer service is powerful marketing.

Why is customer service so important for local businesses?

Primarily, excellent customer service can help local businesses build strong relationships with their customers. By providing personalized attention and going above and beyond to meet customers' needs, local businesses can create a loyal customer base that will keep coming back for more.

Additionally, happy customers are more likely to recommend a business to their friends and family, which can help local businesses grow through word-of-mouth referrals.

In contrast, poor customer service can quickly drive customers away from a business. With social media and online review sites, negative experiences can quickly be shared with a wide audience, which can damage a business's reputation and lead to lost revenue.

Examples of Amazing Customer Service

So what does amazing customer service look like for a local business? Here are a few examples:

1. Personalized Attention

Local businesses have the advantage of being able to offer a more personalized experience for their customers. This can include getting to know customers by name, remembering their preferences, and offering personalized recommendations based on their needs. For example, a local coffee shop might remember a customer's favorite drink and have it ready for them when they walk in the door.

2. Going Above and Beyond

Amazing customer service often involves going beyond to meet customers' needs. This could include offering a complimentary product or service, providing extra assistance, or simply taking the time to listen to a customer's concerns. For example, a local bookstore might offer to order a book for a customer that they do not have in stock, or a local hardware store might guide how to fix a problem at home.

3. Responsiveness

Another important aspect of customer service is responsiveness. When customers have questions or concerns, they want to feel like their business is important to the company they are dealing with. A local business can demonstrate its commitment to customer service by responding promptly to inquiries and providing timely updates.

For example, a local restaurant might respond to a customer's complaint about a bad meal by offering a complimentary dessert or discount on their next visit.

4. Follow-up

Never assume the customer is pleased and will return. Follow-up. This extra step will allow you to truly learn about the customer experience and provide another valuable marketing touch point. Remember how much it costs to acquire a new customer is far more than getting a current customer to buy again. With technology, you can utilize automation with texting, messaging, and phone calls, but never underestimate the tremendous value of personalization.

Turnbow Takeaways on why local businesses need amazing customer service:

1. Excellent customer service can help local businesses build strong relationships with their customers and create a loyal customer base.

2. Poor customer service can quickly damage a business's reputation and lead to lost revenue.

3. Amazing customer service involves providing personalized attention, going above and beyond to meet customers' needs, and being responsive to customer inquiries and concerns.

4. Follow-up. Following up with a customer enables you to truly measure your customer service and simultaneously provides an opportunity to create repeat or additional business.

Ask About WOW Customer Service Training or SALES Training at:

www.JeffTurnbow.com

Chapter 9:
Follow-Through Marketing

Follow-through marketing is the practice of continuously marketing to existing customers after they have made a purchase. This strategy is a critical component of any successful marketing campaign, as it can significantly increase the lifetime value of a customer.

Why is Follow-Through Marketing Important?

Many businesses make the mistake of focusing all their marketing efforts on acquiring new customers. While this is certainly an important aspect of any marketing strategy, it is equally important to focus on retaining and engaging existing customers.

Research has shown that it is significantly less expensive to retain existing customers than it is to acquire new ones.

By consistently marketing to existing customers, businesses can increase their customer retention rates and encourage repeat purchases.

Additionally, happy and engaged customers are more likely to refer their friends and family to a business, which can help to grow a customer base through word-of-mouth referrals.

Ways To Constantly Market to Your Existing Customers

How are you marketing to your existing customers? Here are a few tactics:

1. Email Marketing

Email marketing is still one of the most effective ways to reach out to existing customers. By sending regular newsletters, product updates, and promotions, businesses can stay top of mind with their customers and encourage repeat purchases. Personalization is key in email marketing, as it can increase open rates and click-through rates. By segmenting email lists based on customer interests and purchase history, businesses can send more targeted and relevant messages to their customers.

2. Loyalty Programs

Loyalty programs are still another effective way to encourage repeat purchases. By offering rewards, discounts, or exclusive offers to customers who make repeat purchases or refer new customers, businesses can incentivize their existing customers to continue to engage with their brand.

Loyalty programs can also help businesses collect valuable customer data, such as purchase history and preferences, which can be used to inform future marketing efforts.

3. Social Media Engagement

Social media provides a powerful platform for businesses to engage with their customers and build a community around their brands. By sharing valuable content, responding to customer inquiries and feedback, and hosting promotions or giveaways, businesses can foster strong relationships with their customers and encourage ongoing engagement.

Additionally, social media provides a valuable opportunity for businesses to highlight user-generated content and share customer stories, which can help to build trust and credibility with potential customers.

Growing Your Business Using Follow-Through Marketing

By consistently marketing to existing customers, businesses can increase customer loyalty and encourage repeat purchases. Additionally, engaged, and satisfied customers are more likely to refer new customers to a business, which can help to grow a customer base and increase revenue.

To effectively grow a business through follow-through marketing, businesses should focus on:

1. Consistently engage with customers through email marketing, loyalty programs, texting, phone calls, personal notes, and social media.

2. Personalizing marketing efforts based on customer interests and purchase history.

3. Collecting customer feedback and using it to inform future marketing and product development efforts.

Turnbow Takeaways on follow-through marketing:

1. Follow-through marketing involves consistently marketing to existing customers after they have made a purchase.

2. This strategy can significantly increase customer retention rates and encourage repeat purchases.

3. Businesses can effectively market to existing customers through email marketing, loyalty programs, social media engagement, and personalized marketing efforts.

WHAT CAN YOU START TODAY TO BECOME BETTER AT FOLLOWING UP?

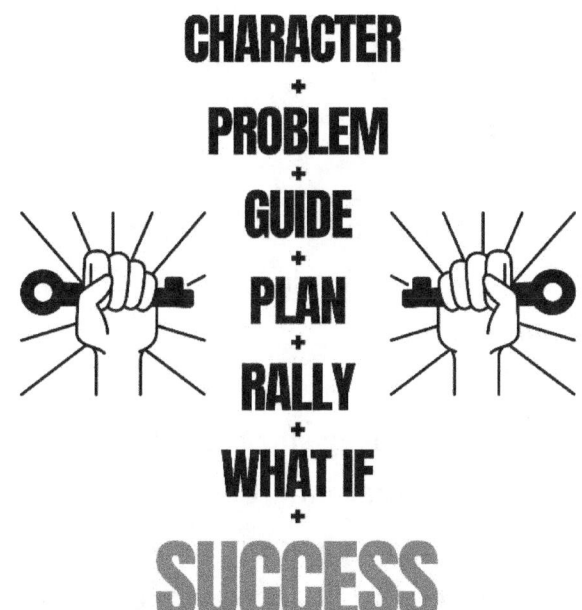

CHARACTER
+
PROBLEM
+
GUIDE
+
PLAN
+
RALLY
+
WHAT IF
+
SUCCESS

Chapter 10:
Storytelling

Storytelling has become an increasingly important aspect of business marketing in recent years.

By telling a compelling story about their brand, businesses can differentiate themselves from the competition, connect with customers on an emotional level, and build a loyal customer base. Here are the top five reasons why storytelling makes a business special, unique, and different from the competition:

1. **Help create an emotional connection with customers.**

Storytelling allows businesses to connect with customers on an emotional level. Customers usually purchase based on emotion. By telling a story that resonates with customers' values and beliefs, businesses can create a sense of loyalty and trust. Emotions play a significant role in purchasing decisions, and a well-crafted story can evoke positive emotions that drive customer loyalty.

2. **Provide a unique brand identity.**

Storytelling can help businesses differentiate themselves from the competition by providing a unique brand identity. A well-told story can capture the essence of a brand's values, personality, and mission, setting it apart from other similar businesses in the marketplace.

3. **Help convey complex ideas.**

Storytelling is an effective way to convey complex ideas in a simple and engaging way. Rather than relying on technical jargon or complex descriptions, businesses can use storytelling to explain the benefits of their products or services in a way that is easy for customers to understand.

4. Builds customer loyalty.

Storytelling is a powerful tool for building customer loyalty. By creating a narrative that aligns with customers' values and beliefs, businesses can create a sense of connection and loyalty that goes beyond simple transactions. Customers who feel a sense of connection with a brand are more likely to become repeat customers and advocates for the brand.

5. Differentiate the brand from the competition.

Storytelling is a way for businesses to differentiate themselves from the competition. By telling a unique story about their brand, businesses can set themselves apart from other businesses in the same industry. This differentiation can help to attract new customers and build a loyal customer base.

The Story Brand Method

Story Brand is a framework developed by Donald Miller to help businesses clarify their message and create a compelling brand narrative that resonates with their customers. The Story Brand Method was based on the premise that every successful brand tells a story that connects with customers on a deep emotional level.

The Story Brand Method consists of seven key elements:

1. **A Character** – The brand should identify with the customer, who is the hero of their own story.

2. **Has a Problem** – The customer has a problem that the brand can help solve.

3. **Meets a Guide** – The brand is positioned as the guide who can help the customer solve their problem.

4. **Who Gives Them a Plan** – The brand provides a clear and actionable plan for the customer to follow.

5. **And Calls Them to Action** – The brand encourages the customer to take action to solve their problem.

6. **That Helps Them Avoid Failure** – The brand emphasizes the negative consequences of not acting.

7. **And Ends in a Success** – The brand helps the customer achieve a successful outcome.

By following these seven elements, businesses can create a clear and compelling narrative that resonates with their customers and motivates them to act. The Story Brand Method can be applied to a wide range of marketing materials, including websites, emails, advertisements, and more.

By following the seven key elements of the Story Brand Method, businesses can create marketing materials that motivate customers to act and ultimately lead to greater success.

US Brands Use Storytelling to Build Customer Loyalty

There are many examples of top USA brands that have built strong customer loyalty through storytelling. Here are a few examples:

1. Apple

Apple is known for its compelling storytelling and its ability to create a sense of community and loyalty among its customers. Apple's marketing campaigns focus on the experience of using its products, rather than just the products themselves. Most buyers do not ask what technology is inside an iPhone. They do not spend hours learning the features, they simply trust the brand and want to be a part of what the brand story has told them.

2. Nike

Nike has built a strong brand identity around the idea of overcoming obstacles and achieving greatness. Through its "Just Do It" campaign, Nike has created a narrative that resonates with customers who are striving to be their best. This has created the impression that if you want to play better, you need Nike.

3. Coca-Cola

Coca-Cola has been telling stories about its brand for over a century. Through its iconic advertising campaigns, Coca-Cola has created a sense of nostalgia and emotion around its products, leading to strong customer loyalty.

4. Harley-Davidson

Harley-Davidson has built a brand around the idea of adventure and freedom. By telling stories about the open road and the sense of community among Harley riders, the company has created a sense of loyalty among its customers.

Turnbow Takeaways on the importance of storytelling in business marketing:

1. Storytelling allows businesses to connect with customers on an emotional level and build customer loyalty.

2. Through storytelling, businesses can differentiate themselves from the competition and create a unique brand identity.

3. Examples of top USA brands with excellent customer loyalty include Apple, Nike, Coca-Cola, and Harley-Davidson.

WE'VE BEEN Winning FOR OVER 20 Years

Chapter 11:
How to Find the Right Marketing Partner

Marketing is a critical aspect of any business, and local businesses often need to seek the help of marketing partners to achieve their marketing goals. However, finding the right marketing partner can be a daunting task. Everyone is selling advertising today. Here are some tips on how to find the right marketing partner for your local business.

Determine Your Marketing Goals

Before you start looking for a marketing partner, you need to determine your marketing goals. What do you want to achieve through your marketing efforts? Are you looking to maintain your status? Looking to open a new business? Do you need help overcoming a major challenge or dominating your market?

The latter will require a partner with vast experience who has demonstrated the ability to manage a strategy from beginning to execution. Also, one who is agile, and able to change to meet the fast changes and demands of today's marketplace.

Consider Your Budget

When it comes to marketing, you get what you pay for. A low-cost marketing partner may seem like an attractive option, but they may not be able to deliver the results you need. Consider your budget carefully and look for a marketing partner who can deliver the results you need within your budget. A great marketer understands the value of their time and the time you will need as well. They will usually negotiate a budget that works for you both.

Choose a Partner with Real World Experience

Real-world business growth experience matters. Seek a partner who has taken on the challenges you are pursuing. A marketing partner with experience achieving your goals will be able to develop and execute a marketing strategy that is tailored to your specific needs.

When it comes to managing your business's marketing strategy, you have three primary options: hiring an in-house marketing manager or outsourcing to a fractional CMO – or a hybrid.

A fractional CMO is someone with the experience to be a chief marketing officer but only charges for the fraction of time spent on your business. They usually work closely with a few select businesses and function more like an employee without the full costs of an employee. Both options have their benefits and drawbacks, and the best choice depends on your business's unique needs and resources.

In-House Marketing Manager

An in-house marketing manager is a full-time employee who is responsible for developing and executing your business's marketing strategy. They work directly for your business and are integrated into your team. Some benefits of hiring an in-house marketing manager include:

1. **Dedicated focus on your business:** An in-house marketing manager can devote their full attention to your business's marketing needs and can work closely with other departments to ensure that all marketing efforts are aligned with your business goals.

2. **Knowledge of your industry and business:** An in-house marketing manager has an intimate understanding of your business's products, services, customers, and industry. This knowledge can inform the development of a tailored marketing strategy that fits your business's unique needs.

3. **Control and oversight:** With an in-house marketing manager, you have direct control and oversight over your

marketing strategy. You can closely monitor their progress, provide feedback, and make changes as needed.

Fractional CMO

A fractional CMO is an outsourced chief marketing officer who works with your business on a part-time or project basis. They provide strategic guidance, oversee the development and execution of your marketing plan, and help you achieve your business goals. Some benefits of outsourcing your marketing strategy to a fractional CMO include:

1. **Access to expertise:** A fractional CMO brings a wealth of experience and expertise to your business without the prohibitive cost of a full-time executive. They can provide strategic guidance, develop a marketing plan, and oversee the execution of your marketing initiatives.

2. **Cost-effective:** Outsourcing your marketing strategy to a fractional CMO is often more cost-effective than hiring an in-house marketing manager. You only pay for the services you need, and you do not have to worry about the cost of benefits, training, and other expenses associated with hiring a full-time employee.

3. **Flexible and scalable:** With a fractional CMO, you have the flexibility to scale your marketing efforts up or down as needed. They can work on a project-by-project basis, or you can engage them for ongoing support. This flexibility makes it easy to adjust your marketing strategy as your business needs change.

In conclusion, both hiring an in-house marketing manager and outsourcing to a fractional CMO have their benefits. The choice between the two depends on your business's unique needs, budget, and resources. You could go with a hybrid model – a fractional CMO could be the strategist, budgeting manager, and focus on areas like optimization whereas the marketing director or in-house team focuses more on the execution of the plan.

Your **Turnbow Takeaways**:

1. Find a partner who understands your business needs and has experience reaching similar goals.

2. Keep your budget in mind and make sure their plan gives you an ROI that makes it easy to cover all their costs.

3. Exclusivity – You deserve better than a cookie-cutter marketing program. Seek out someone who will not assist your competition while they work with you.

You deserve their full attention. **(Turnbow offers this. He works with one client per industry per market area).**

4. Look beyond what the partner will do immediately, and how their service will continue to be successful. Are they bringing assets and resources into your business? Do they expand your capabilities? Is this someone you see working with you for many years to come?

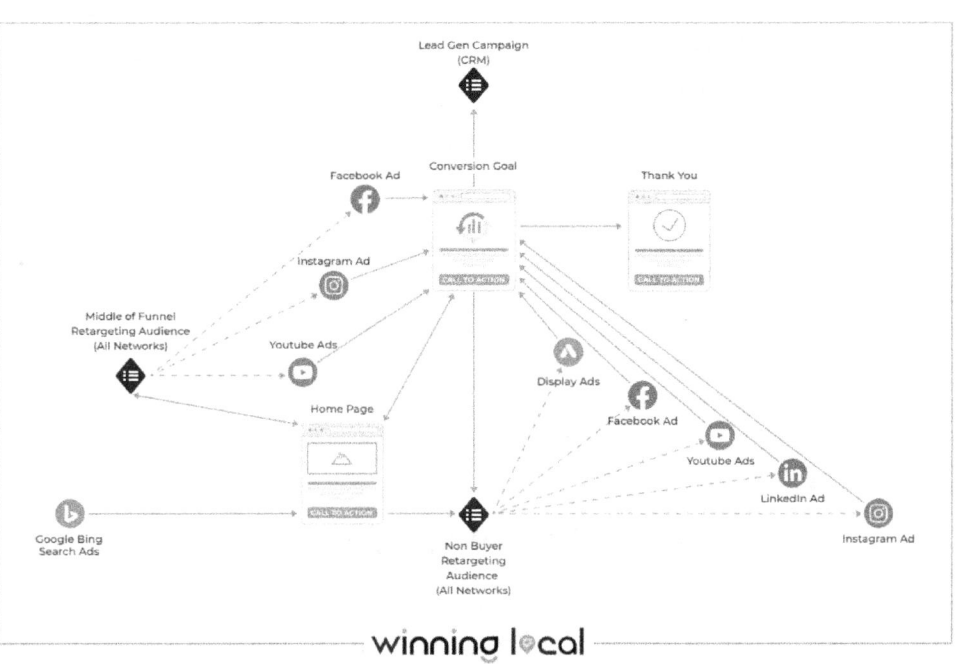

Lead Gen Campaign (CRM)

Facebook Ad

Conversion Goal

Thank You

Instagram Ad

Middle of Funnel Retargeting Audience (All Networks)

Youtube Ads

Home Page

Display Ads

Facebook Ad

Youtube Ads

LinkedIn Ad

Google Bing Search Ads

Non Buyer Retargeting Audience (All Networks)

Instagram Ad

winning local

First, what is the goal?
Lead Generation?
Awareness?
Loyalty?

Chapter 12:
Top Go-to Marketing Tactics

One of the biggest challenges for small businesses is deciding which marketing tactic is best. They are constantly bombarded with sales pitches about the latest and greatest marketing tactic.

Right now, there are at least 20 marketing tactics that seem like great ideas to most business owners. However, if you charge ahead fully with each marketing tactic without a sufficient budget, you are using what I call a diluted strategy. A diluted strategy is when the business is doing many things and not doing a few things great and with significant impact. I have a visual example that I show my clients:

Imagine having a pitcher of water to represent your budget.

We start there because your budget will determine how many tactics we can afford to utilize. Now imagine a table with 20 cups to represent all the marketing tactics.

If you drip a bit of water into each cup, then none is full. All are weak. A better approach is to do the homework to decide which marketing tactic will work best for your specific goals. Choose the number of cups that you can completely fill with your budget. Pour your budget, design, and supporting marketing efforts into those tactics and make them have the most impact possible. That is how you stop wasting your budget and make more of a concentrated impact with what you can afford to spend.

What are the top Go-to Tactics?

Did you know that recent estimates show that the average person sees upwards of 4,000 ads per day? Many people develop a sort of "advertising overload" where they subconsciously filter out ads they're seeing, especially online. This is another reason the diluted strategy is ineffective and inefficient marketing.

This is a common problem as many businesses try to advertise in many places or with many tactics and therefore their message is not focused and doesn't provide the repetition required to get attention and create action.

Think of a new pizza launch. Let's use BBQ pizza (which I think is awful) ha! The first time I see that ad I will not give it much thought. The third time I see the ad, I think "Hmmm, interesting", but the 7th time I see that ad and how delicious they make it look, I am thinking "Maybe I should give it a try". Now, imagine if the pizza company changes its creative back to pepperoni. All that effort was just wasted because I was near the point of taking action to try that pizza. Great pizza marketers know this. They know how many times a consumer needs to see the ad before they act and buy.

What's even better? If they keep promoting that BBQ pizza ad to those who already like pizza, and I order it often, then I am very likely to give it a try earlier.

Now they have data to know that I ordered BBQ pizza one time but also that I order Pineapple and Pepperoni most often. Their data will show that I will try new pizzas, but I am most loyal to a certain type of pizza. They are now equipped to market new pizzas to me as well as my favorite pizza.

So, how can they afford to show me that 7-10 times? Because they are not usually showing it to everyone who eats - they start their focus by showing it most often to their customer base by uploading their CRM to the campaign or they are showing it to people who often order pizza. From here, they can now drill down to their popular neighborhoods. This makes their budget more focused and allows them to show the right people the right ad with just the right amount of frequency.

Creative vs. Directional Advertising

For any business, you will need tactics for creative and directional advertising. Creative advertising simply places messages out there to your target audience and encourages them to buy or act. It creates awareness. Directional advertising is the tactic of making certain that you are an option where and when buyers are ready to act. The more budget you have, the more of these options you can choose. **However, let us start with the top 2:**

Facebook/ Instagram (Meta) and Google.

Most people spend most of their time here. Some reports indicate most spend 6 hours per day on Facebook alone!

I know that so many businesses have grown frustrated with Facebook/Instagram and this happens usually for these reasons: the platform makes it appear easy to use for business; the business uses a throwing darts strategy. Nevertheless, Meta is powerful. They allow you to use display ads or videos on one platform to two tactics.

Another reason for the frustration is that when Facebook went public, they had to begin focusing on profit growth to their shareholders and this changed the small business marketing capabilities significantly.

Considering this, the more experienced and focused Facebook/Instagram marketer will get the best results. If you are a do-it-yourself, here is a great tip. Start with targeting. You can link your Instagram and Facebook, so the ads run on both platforms simultaneously. Know your audience and know that the platforms have slightly different users, and they use them a bit differently.

Use as much of the targeting as possible. Now create two ads that give a great call to action. Set up targeting and run both ads for about $3 per day for 7 days. What? Trust me - test first.

Now evaluate which is performing better. Now, double the spend on the best-performing ad and try it for another 7 days. If the results are increasing you can increase that spend and reevaluate after 30 days for return on investment. Yes, this seems like a protracted process, but the best campaigns are tested first and run longer so the frequency of the message has enough time to create awareness, interest, consideration, and action. If you have a teenage audience, you can incorporate platforms like TikTok (I do not personally recommend TikTok), Snapchat, or focus more on Instagram.

Google: Directional Advertising

Social is where most people gain interest in a product or service. However, it is becoming a directional form of advertising as well by allowing easy searches and purchases on the platform. This could be the only tactical option you need- again depending on your goals and budget.

Google built its platform to be the place where people go when they are researching and/or ready to buy.

With Google, you can get your business placed in front of those looking for information and those ready to buy.

65% of searchers click paid ads. These tend to be the higher intent buyers in the 'ready to buy' stage. They have usually performed their research and they know these are paid ads selling what they want.

It is imperative to be an option when someone is ready to buy, therefore paid ads should be a top priority. You will see Google change its platform again soon to allow even easier purchasing decisions during the search.

Google has made it easy to purchase your advertising campaign on its platform. Once again, the more experienced marketer is going to get you the best results. However, if you must do it yourself, you can run your campaign on their platform.

I would only recommend this do-it-yourself to someone who has $800 or less to spend per month and they have an exceedingly small geographic area focus. If you are spending more than $800 per month, you will benefit by getting an experienced marketer using a time-tested automation system along with their skills to manage this campaign.

Yes, they will make a profit, thereby seemingly reducing your budget to Google, but they can get you more results with less budget going to Google through efficiencies, experience, and strategy.

Top Tips for Paid Google Search

According to several PPC experts, the most important tip for improving search advertising is to set appropriate and achievable goals for your campaign. To do this, businesses need to determine their ultimate objective and build their strategy around it. Each company has unique customer acquisition strategies, target customers, and budgets that need to be considered when setting goals.

Secondly, running search ads across multiple platforms, such as Bing and Google, can improve conversion rates and provide more opportunities for clicks and conversions. I've had many businesses tell me they don't care about Bing, but consider this:

Searchers on Bing tend to convert more often, cost far less per click, and are usually an upper-income demographic - so, don't forget Bing! While their volume of searchers is lower than Google, their quality and the cost to get them are much lower. You want all the buyers, right?

Finally, it is essential to select the right budget for paid search advertising campaigns, which may take time and require investments. Small businesses should be realistic about their expectations and not assume instant success, particularly with limited budgets or low-volume keywords.

Again, those are the two go-to tactics for most businesses. However, there are so many others such as: SEO; Retargeting; Geo-fencing; Conquesting competitors, Targeted TV, Targeted radio; Direct Mail; Email; and so many more. This is why it is vital to take marketing as seriously as the location and quality of your business and work with someone who can steer your marketing engine appropriately and the most effectively.

You may seem to spend more, but at the end of the day, it is the return on investment that matters. If you get back more than you spend, and significantly, you will gladly spend the budget and increase it to keep increasing your results. Oh, and you will reduce your stress and increase your ability to focus on running your business.

Website Conversion Rate Optimization

Driving traffic to websites is the main focus of most marketing teams, hoping that this traffic will convert into qualified leads for sales representatives to close. However, hope is not a strategy. This approach is only half the battle. You will achieve long-term, sustainable growth by getting more out of existing traffic and leads first, and this is where web conversion rate optimization (CRO) comes into play.

CRO is the process of increasing the percentage of users or website visitors who complete a specific action to generate more leads. This can be achieved through content enhancements, split testing, and workflow improvement., The results are more highly qualified leads, increased revenue, and lower acquisition costs.

To improve conversions, it is essential to understand how visitors should convert and test it. For example, if you want phone calls, make sure your phone number is located prominently throughout the website. Begin the website layout with the end goal in mind and focus on building the site to drive visitors to act. Other ways to convert traffic include adding a chat or text feature, creating a pop-up box that provides value, and retargeting visitors with online ads.

Retargeting - Advertising Insurance

Retargeting works by tracking visitors to your website or another location and serving them online ads as they surf around the web. By leveraging retargeting on Facebook and other platforms, companies can re-engage people who left the website, and this is particularly impactful when retargeting those who visited the highest-converting web pages. Using tools like heatmaps can identify where the audience goes on the website, and A/B testing can be used to adjust the site to get visitors to take the desired action. We know that 95-98% of first-time visitors do not act. Discouraging, I know! However, we know that a return visitor is 3-4 times more likely to take action.

That is why I refer to Retargeting as Advertising Insurance. Retargeting visitors to your site only maximizes your cost of getting them to your site. By following these visitors once they leave, you increase and expedite their return, therefore your return on investment simultaneously.

Turnbow Takeaways:

1. Always start with a test budget before you start spending your full amount.

2. Pay careful attention to the stats and continually work to improve your conversion rate.

3. Consider starting with retargeting to recoup the traffic who have already visited your website.

4. Do NOT forget your foundation. Your GMB profile, Optimize your Google Maps Listings, Optimize your site and social media channels, and make certain that your site is optimized for SEO before you begin.

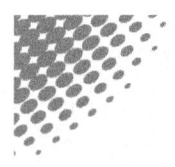

WINNING ISN'T EASY.
HOWEVER,
WINNING BECOMES EASIER
WHEN IT BECOMES A

habit.

Chapter 13:
Prepare Your Team

I struggled with making this the first chapter.

Your team is your greatest asset or liability. I love everything about the Zig Ziglar philosophies of business! One of his quotes is: The only thing worse than training employees and losing them is to not train them and keep them.

I understand the frustration of turnover and constantly training employees who eventually leave. Unfortunately, this is a part of doing business and an especially important part of successful businesses. Continuous training and motivation are essential to happy, helpful, employees.

Sales Training is Required.

A big misconception is that sales training teaches your employees to simply push your products and services onto your customers. Instead, great sales training will equip your team to discover the needs and wants of your customers and help them make decisions better and faster.

I have learned many sales practices, but my favorite is using the Sandler Sales Institute style of consultative selling. Since that training, I have created a system to incorporate similar techniques and updated my training to meet the needs and desires of today's consumers. When I perform sales training for my client, I customize it based on my client's unique goals. My goal is to help your team communicate better, become your unique brand ambassador, and become infused with the overall marketing strategy. My **WOW Customer Service** Training coaches teams how to deliver an experience that helps you dominate your market area. Sales and Customer Service are critical components of marketing and often go unrealized by marketers.

When I think of marketing, I believe everyone on the team should know how to move the business forward in one mind and accord.

Training Topics: Service That Sells.

Great Customer Service skills include much more than being friendly.

Often businesses do not invest in training, and it creates a big breakdown in their overall marketing and growth. Your people are a vital part of your marketing plan and in many cases the last step of your marketing plan when action happens. It would not be wise to invest in a marketing strategy only to neglect the final stage, right?

Service That Sells teaches that selling is like being a great listener, matchmaker, and servant to the potential customer. Rather than trying to get someone to decide, this philosophy helps the customer reach their desired decision more quickly and with ease.

Training Topics: Motivation

It is much more than cheerleading. Now, more than ever, people require motivation to be successful.

According to PositivePsychology.com Motivation reflects something unique about each one of us and allows us to gain valued outcomes like improved performance, enhanced well-being, personal growth, or a sense of purpose. Motivation is a pathway to change our way of thinking, feeling, and behaving.

We know through studies that motivated employees are more loyal and dedicated to the company's goals. Motivation builds something fiercely competitive - determination. It is exceedingly difficult to beat a determined company. The more determined the company becomes, the harder it is to beat them. A determined team has purpose, passion, direction, focus, and confidence.

Just like David in the David and Goliath story, David was bold and determined, and sometimes just being able and intentionally prepared to show up as a winner is more than 80% of the battle. Ask yourself, who wins: The company with the determined, passionate, and well-trained team or the one without motivation and determination or direction? Easy call, right?

Training Topics: **Marketing and Sales - The Engine**

Many times, marketing and sales can come at odds with each other. Tensions can build and blame can be pointed back and forth. This is often a result of poor communication and team building. Sales should be involved and educated about the marketing strategy to the point where they understand they are the valuable component of the overarching strategy. They should feel like one team.

I have learned that communication, often, resolves this tension and creates a constructive interaction between these two departments. Communication and engagement between these departments should be encouraged and it should happen often.

Turnbow Takeaways:

1. Invest in training your people. There is no greater investment than improving the people who are working for you.

2. Invest in yourself, so you are the best leader you can be. Most people are motivated by more than just money. Most are motivated by having a sense of purpose, respect, and value to the organization.

3. Motivation is a pathway to change our way of thinking, feeling, and behaving.

Chapter 14:
Real-Life Davids Taking on Goliaths

To gain a competitive advantage, entrepreneurs must think creatively and disrupt traditional industry norms. Innovation, whether in the form of innovative technology or a new business model, has the potential to level the playing field and allow smaller companies to compete with larger ones.

Persistence is also required to overcome obstacles and achieve success. Entrepreneurs must stay focused on their goals and have the courage to take risks and keep trying even when they face setbacks.

The story of David and Goliath is more than just a religious historical story. It is a timeless story that can inspire us in all aspects of our lives, including business. Small businesses can achieve remarkable success by embracing creativity, persistence, determination, and the courage to take on larger competitors.

1. Ben & Jerry's

The story of David and Goliath serves as a powerful metaphor for the story of Ben & Jerry's ice cream company. Ben & Jerry's began as a small company with two founders who were enthusiastic about making high-quality ice cream.

Ben Cohen and Jerry Greenfield decided to enroll in an ice cream-making class for $5. By 1978, the two aspiring entrepreneurs had saved up $12,000 to convert a renovated petrol station into their first store, and Ben & Jerry's was born.

Joel Chery notes that just two years later, the pair began distributing their growing brand from the back of Cohen's Volkswagen to local grocers and small corner stores.

Häagen-Dazs attempted but failed to prevent the duo from distributing their products in the Boston area. Ben & Jerry's was sold to Unilever for $326 million after two decades in business.

2. Apple Inc.

Apple Inc. is a technology behemoth that can be compared to a Goliath in the industry, dominating markets and wielding enormous power. However, the story of David and Goliath can still be applied to Apple, as the company was once a scrappy underdog that defeated industry titans.

According to Joel Chery, Apple is one of the most famous underdog stories. In 1976, college dropouts Steve Jobs and Steve Wozniak (along with a third partner who sold his share of the company within the first three months) founded Apple.

Since 1976, Apple has evolved into the multinational technology behemoth that it is today. After Samsung and Huawei, Apple is now the world's largest information technology company by revenue and the world's third-largest mobile phone manufacturer.

3. Netflix

Netflix is a prime example of a company that has successfully taken on industry giants to become a Goliath itself. The company started as a small DVD-by-mail service and faced fierce competition from industry leader Blockbuster.

Blockbuster turned down a $50 million offer to buy Netflix in the early 2000s, and soon after announced bankruptcy and the closure of 9,000 stores worldwide. (Except for one store in Bend, Oregon.)

The innovative streaming service had 50 million subscribers by 2014 and had won seven Emmy Awards.

4. Cliff-Bar

Clif Bar is a company that embodies David's triumph over Goliath. Gary Erickson founded the company in 1992 when the energy bar market was dominated by large players such as PowerBar.

It was nothing short of a miracle that he had received such an offer, given that only eight years prior he had been working long hours at a garage to make ends meet and was the owner of a tiny, unprofitable bakery.

Erickson had the idea for an energy bar after a 175-mile bike ride one day, and it took off. He began making and selling the bars from his mother's kitchen and has experienced double-digit compound growth for over a decade.

5. Five Guys

According to legend, Jerry Murrel wanted a job that would keep his family close by and, of course, pay well. What is the solution? Jerry and his sons agreed to use their college funds to start a burger restaurant.

Competing with McDonald's and Burger King is an arduous task for anyone; their prices are simply unbeatable. But Jerry understood their standard could be (easily) surpassed. Murrel and his sons founded Five Guys Burgers and Fries with recipes for superior-quality burgers and fries.

Yes, McDonald's is cheaper and faster, and that works in today's fast-paced world. Five Guys, on the other hand, isn't afraid to tell their customers that they might have to wait a little longer, because the wait will be worth it for a quality burger.

Turnbow Takeaways:

1. Creativity and innovation are key to taking on larger competitors in business. Just as David used his slingshot to defeat Goliath, smaller companies can disrupt industries and achieve success by embracing new ideas and approaches.

2. Standing up for one's values and beliefs can also be a valuable success tool. For example, Ben & Jerry's has built a loyal customer base by advocating for social and environmental causes. As a result, the company has distinguished itself from its competitors and established a strong brand identity.

3. With the right strategy and mindset, even Goliaths can be defeated. Apple and Netflix were once considered underdogs, but they

were able to disrupt industries and achieve success by embracing innovation, creativity, and a willingness to take risks. The story of David and Goliath serves as a reminder that smaller businesses can compete with larger competitors and win if they take the right approach.

4. It is challenging to imagine these companies as underdogs, right? Your idea can be just as big. Your company can be just as influential in the space you are working. You don't want to be a Goliath? That's ok, too. Maybe you just want to win your fair share of your local market.
Determining your goals and vision is the key and the beginning of charting your individual definition of success.

178

Chapter 15:
How to Work with The Man Who Wrote the Book on Winning Local

Jeff Turnbow founded his company over 20 years ago. It evolved from a small agency that would take on any client willing to pay, to a more relational business model. Turnbow has personally advised over 3,000 diverse businesses throughout his career.

"We stay ahead of all advanced marketing tools, and we have decades of relationships within the industry," Turnbow says. "This provides the know-how and partnerships to accomplish extraordinary goals quickly." He founded his company to "help the underdog - I love that!"

"The small business community is the backbone of our society, but they frequently lack the necessary resources and authentic partnerships to effectively achieve their vision."

Jeff was recently chosen as one of 25 professionals to write a chapter for a book compilation edited by Jack Canfield, author of "Chicken Soup for the Soul." Turnbow's chapter won the editor's choice award, and the book made four best-seller lists on Amazon.com.

He was voted Best Marketing Consultant in Arkansas by the readers of the state's largest publication. His training includes certifications from Google, Harvard, Cornell, LinkedIn, and more. Turnbow has been hired by top media companies and many universities to train or lead in the areas of sales and marketing.

He is the most invited returning speaker and emcee for the world's largest digital marketing conference series.

Recently, Jeff was invited to Emcee and teach master classes at digital marketing conferences across Europe. He spoke at London, Dublin, Barcelona, and Amsterdam. While he is honored to be a speaker and emcee at these incredible events, Jeff loves the ability to also sit and listen to other thought leaders and gain the winning edge to help his clients.

Jeff is passionate about growing small businesses and understands that he must keep his toolbox full and his capabilities sharp. His approach to his clients is unique. Jeff gets to know his client's goals, strengths, weaknesses, and nuances of their business. He takes the steps other companies will not or do not. He is diligent at winning.

How can you work with Jeff Turnbow?

1. Get a FREE Analysis of your online business - Are you Winning?
   Get 5 quick easy changes that will greatly impact your sales.

2. Get a FREE Website Conversion Optimization Session to convert more of your current visitors into action.

3. Work with his agency – Winning Local

4. Bring Turnbow in as your consultant or Fractional Chief Marketing Officer at a fraction of the expense it would cost to hire this level of employee.

5. Request Business Coaching Services - Weekly Power Hours to level up your entire strategy and execution to increase profits.

6. Get your team better equipped by Training Services with Turnbow. The most requested topics are Sales Training, Customer Service That Sells, and Motivating Your Team to Win! All training comes with a 100% Satisfaction Guarantee.

Visit www.WinningLocal.com for web design, advertising, or marketing services.

Visit www.JeffTurnbow.com for business coaching, consulting, or working with Jeff as your Marketing Director or CMO.

Also, you may Call / Text Jeff at 501-505-6278 to start communicating one on one.

AI and Additional Free Resources

Case Studies

AI and Resources

AI – Artificial Intelligence
(Written by Bing Chat using the prompt: what is AI, how can it be used in marketing, and give examples of free tools)

AI, short for **artificial intelligence**, is the intelligence demonstrated by machines or software. It is the field of study in computer science that develops and studies intelligent machines[1234]. AI enables computers to perform tasks commonly associated with intelligent beings, such as reasoning, discovering meaning, generalizing, or learning from past experiences[2].

AI has found its application in various domains, including marketing. It has the potential to enhance marketing activities by understanding customer needs, matching them to products and services, and persuading people to buy[5]. Some of the ways AI can be used for marketing include:

- **Chatbots**: AI-powered chatbots can assist with lead development, customer support, cross-selling, or upselling[5].
- **Inbound call analysis**: AI can analyze and route inbound calls to appropriate departments[5].
- **Digital ad placement**: AI can handle digital ad placement tasks, also known as "programmatic buying"[5].
- **Enhancing predictions**: AI can assist in enhancing the accuracy of predictions, such as sales forecasts[5].
- **Content optimization**: AI can optimize marketing assets like chatbots, targeted advertising, and content generation[6].

As for free AI tools, here are some examples you can explore:

1. **ChatGPT**: A tool that uses AI to generate human-like text responses[7].
2. **Quillbot**: An AI-powered writing assistant that helps paraphrase and improve text[7].

3. **Hivemind**: A tool that enables collaborative brainstorming using AI-generated prompts[7].
4. **DALL·E 2**: An open-source image generator that uses artificial intelligence[8].
5. **WOMBO**: An AI-powered app that brings photos to life with singing and dancing[7].

Please note that the availability and functionality of these tools may vary over time. It is always a good idea to check their respective websites for the most up-to-date information.

Let me know if there is anything else I can help you with!

How could I have said it better? haha

AI can be used alongside any chapter in this book. We use it daily and have been using automation for over 15 years. One of the most important steps in learning how to utilize AI is to begin trying different types and learning how to write proper prompts for the best results.

This was a quick demo for the purpose of adding AI in this book. AI will evolve in 2024 and I predict it will make marketers who use it more effective and more efficient. It will not, at this point, replace the intelligence of a human marketer with years of knowledge of learning strategies that do and do not work for marketing businesses.

ZOHO: Customer Relationship Management

ZOHO Customer Relationship Management (CRM) is a software platform made for business management which includes interactions with customers for more efficient sales processes. It is loaded with features both basic and advanced that are optimized for enterprises of many sizes. It can be especially useful for customer relationships, sales processes streamline, and business expansion.

Wave: Accounting / Invoicing

Wave is a cloud-based software platform that gives useful accounting and invoicing tools for small enterprises. With the help of this tool, entrepreneurs will be able to have more efficient fiscal management and reports of their day-to-day operations. The platform is free to use for accounting and invoicing. Income and expenses are also trackable according to their classifications. Issue recurring invoices and receiving payments online are also made possible.

Legal Zoom: Legal help for small businesses

LegalZoom is a software platform founded in 2001. It offers legal help and documentation services for small businesses and individuals. The services include formation and incorporation, trademark registration, business compliance, legal document review, and registered agent services. Access to various licensed attorneys for consultation sessions is also made available.

Bambee: HR for Small Businesses

Bambee is a software platform that allows small businesses to enjoy various human resources services. Since 2016, it has helped a vast number of business owners with HR management. The services that they offer include employee onboarding, compliance management, policy creation and implementation, performance management, termination support, and HR consulting.

Square or Clover POS systems

Square and Clover are both known point-of-sale systems that are very efficient for small and medium-sized enterprises for their sales management. They offer handy features such as the ability to accept a variety of payment types, manage inventory, track sales, and more.

Case Studies

I have listed a few case studies to demonstrate how these philosophies and strategies work for local businesses. These are real examples of Winning Local. However, out of respect to our clients, we will not disclose trade secrets and proprietary information. These case studies show valuable details, but they do not disclose all the strategies and tactics used to obtain these significant success stories.

Southaven RV and Marine

What Were the Actual Results?

Since we led all aspects of the marketing strategy for Southaven RV and Marine, the results have been astounding. The company has seen over a 500% percent growth in leads over the past several years, as well as over 100% growth in profits.

While our competition was focused on metrics such as time on site and traffic volume, we narrowed our focus to improved metrics such as time to convert, conversion rate optimization, quality traffic, and quality lead generation.

We did this while simultaneously giving the shopper the tools and content they desired based on research in the industries.

Our Goal

From day one, our goal with Southaven RV and Marine was to update their web presence and expand their sales. We carefully listened to the CEO and executed his vision for his company.

We were able to do this by leveraging tactics in website conversion optimization, content marketing, paid search, SEO, social media marketing, and a cross-channel consumer-focused marketing strategy. By focusing the tactics on the most likely buyers, we were able to rapidly increase leads and revenues.

How Did We Do This?

Complete Rebranding

From the logo to the website, to the online and offline marketing, we updated everything to use the new messaging. We positioned their 130,000-square-foot showroom as a key differentiator for consumers looking for an RV or Boat. We realized through research that competitors offer their products outdoors - many in extreme climates and this is uncomfortable for the shopping experience. Southaven RV and Marine evolved from a local store to America's Largest RV and Marine Indoor Superstore.

Lead Generation-Focused Website

We updated the entire online experience to focus on meeting the needs of our target audience in a more personalized and creative way to retain customers.

We utilized heat maps and A/B testing to redesign the website for optimal experiences across all devices. We continuously look for ways to reduce the number of clicks for the shopper and convert them into a one-on-one conversation with one of their well-trained consultants.

The Future

We developed messages and goals and continuously shared them with all departments. We involved the employees to buy in for these new goals of becoming a more innovative shopping center for local, regional, and national buyers alike. The CEO will determine the future goals. I see us moving into more utilization of AI technologies and rebranding to become a national brand leader. I also see other opportunities to create niche companies that will serve their ultimate mission.

Dr. Carmella Knoernschild, Orthodontist

What Were the Actual Results?

Revenues grew 7X.

Profits grew 5X.

Brand presence went from strong to dominant.

Since we led all aspects of the marketing strategy for Dr. Carmell Knoernschild, the results have been exponential year over year. Before we engaged, the marketing lacked focused messaging and tactical strategy. We moved the budget from newspaper to online and developed a focused strategy to communicate our message to mothers and kids/teens. We redesigned the web presence using conversion-based optimization, improved content, added more video messaging, and launched a very targeted yet very dominant brand awareness campaign. We achieved the results without increasing their overall marketing spend.

Our Goal

From day one, we recognized the superior level of training and expertise in our client compared to the competition. We restyled the brand to communicate her client-given nickname, thereby making her brand easier to recall. We focused on her expertise and key differentiators and delivered that messaging with the appropriate frequency utilizing a cross-channel marketing strategy.

We realized the unique marketplace lacked Google searches for intended buyers and leveraged social media to reach our target audiences. We utilized captivating videos to build her community brand while telling her story of expertise and superiority in Orthodontics.

How Did We Do This?

Complete Rebranding from the logo to the website, the online and offline marketing. We updated everything to use the new messaging. We developed specific messaging and the appropriate frequency across multiple channels. We helped her develop a children's book, sponsored local teams, helped her win awards, and catapulted her expertise and unique training and capabilities. The awards and recognition remain as content easy to find.

Lead Generation-Focused Website

We updated the entire online experience to focus on meeting the needs of our target audience in a more personalized and creative way to retain customers.

We utilized heat maps and A/B testing to redesign the website for optimal experiences across all devices. We continuously look for ways to reduce the number of clicks for the shopper and convert them into an easier online booking experience.

Re-envisioned The Future

We developed promotions, messages, and goals and continuously shared this with all departments. We involved the entire company to buy in for new goals of displaying their already innovative practice and encouraged changes to increase new patient capacity.

Focused Content Marketing and Reviews

We focused on creating content quickly, that could be easily multi-purposed uniquely in different media. We helped increase patient reviews and create fun ways to promote happy patients throughout the market area.

THERE'S MARKETING,
THEN THERE'S *Winning!*

C & D Drug Store

What Were the Actual Results?

Brand presence grew to market dominance in comparison to similar locally owned pharmacies as well as big box pharmacies. Deliveries grew over 500%, requiring multiple car purchases to manage deliveries. Revenues grew over 100%. Two major chains came into the marketplace and our client was able to grow despite their presence and one closed shortly after opening.

Rather than having a negative impact on our clients, online orders increased by over 200%. Refill requests increased by over 400%. New clients switched pharmacies to our clients by making the process easy and incredibly attractive.

Our Goal

From day one, our client seemed to worry about their location and aging customer base as a weakness. We identified their unique capabilities and developed a strategy of communicating these strengths better, launching online orders and free delivery services. This would counter the location weakness and attract current demographics as well as younger demographics to the pharmacy.

We realized this unique marketplace lacked Google searches for intended buyers and therefore leveraged more creative awareness on social media and targeted radio to reach our target audiences. We produced many captivating videos but one was styled similar to the famous MAC vs. PC to create a David vs Goliath wow moment in the community. We positioned the brand uniquely from other independent pharmacies while simultaneously attacking the big box pharmacies at their weaknesses - delivery - custom compounding - and curbside-friendly services. We did this by redirecting their marketing budget without increasing it.

Complete Rebranding

From the logo to the website to the online and offline marketing, we refreshed everything to use the new messaging. We developed specific messaging and the appropriate frequency across multiple channels.

David Vs. Goliath

We researched the competition and built a strategy around their weaknesses and our client's strengths. We studied competitive marketing tactics and we found niche areas to deliver our message more efficiently and more frequently. We developed and utilized our Zig-While-They-Zag-Strategy.

CONCLUSION

Thank you for taking the time to read this book. It is my goal that you gain a few nuggets of value that will help you obtain the level of success that is right for you.

Full-service marketing agency owned by Jeff Turnbow: www.WinningLocal.com

Collaborate directly with me as a consultant, speaker, trainer, coach, or fractional CMO: Visit www.JeffTurnbow.com

Jeff Turnbow

THANK YOU!

Jeremiah 29:11

"Success is getting what you want.
Happiness is wanting what you get."
Dale Carnegie

www.ingramcontent.com/pod-product-compliance
Lightning Source LLC
Chambersburg PA
CBHW072153290526
45794CB00004B/1507